MW01054049

Title: Quick Pick Old Time Banjo for the Absolute Beginner
Subtitle: A Quick Start Method to Playing "Up-Picking",
an Easy to Learn Old Time Style of Banjo Playing.
Copyright © 2010 Anna E. Uptain

Title ID: 3687173
ISBN-13: 978-1466320802

Table of Contents

Audio Examples for the Book can be found at:
www.fretsalive.com

Tuning Your Banjo

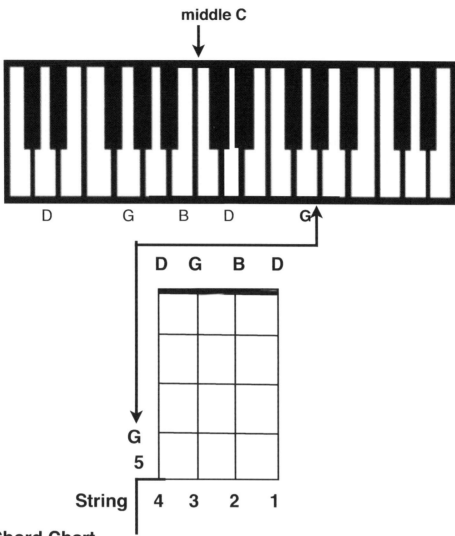

Reading a Chord Chart

Chord charts are read as if you are looking directly at the front of the banjo. The top, or darkest, line represents the white bar or "nut" at the top of the banjo fretboard (the part of the instrument where you place your fingers to make chords). Each vertical line represents a banjo string, starting with the 4th and largest/lowest-sounding string on the far left, to the 1st and smallest/highest-sounding string on the right. The 5th string is even higher sounding; it is shorter than the rest and is tuned last to high G. Each horizontal line represents one of the gold lines that go across your fretboard; the spaces between the lines are called frets. The frets show where to put your finger. The circles show which string to put your finger on, and the number in the circle shows which finger to use (1 for index, 2 for second finger, 3 for ring finger, and 4 for your "pinky" finger).

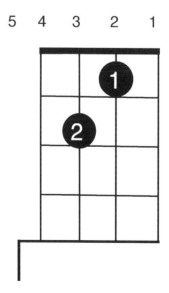

Deciding Whether Or Not To Use Picks

For the up-picking style of playing the banjo, you will need only one thumb pick and one metal finger pick, which is placed on your index finger. Picks are optional for this style of playing, but it's suggested that you use them until you become familiar with the technique.

Picks make it easier to "pick up" or "pull" the strings individually, and they provide a louder sound. Some folks have a hard time getting accustomed to picks, and they prefer to use their bare fingers. This is a personal preference; keep in mind that your banjo will lose some volume if you play without picks.

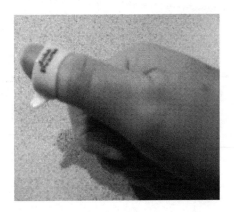

Thumb picks come in sizes S to XL, so try several to make sure you get a snug fit. Most folks use plastic thumb picks, which are easier to size. Metal thumb picks are also available.

Metal finger picks are available in S to XL sizes; they are also available in gauges. For beginners, recommended gauges are .018 or .020. As you become more comfortable using a pick, you'll find the size that suits you the best. (As a woman, I prefer the .013 gauge because they are smaller and easier to mold to my fingers.)

**Note that with the "up picking" style, you will only need a thumb pick and an index finger pick.

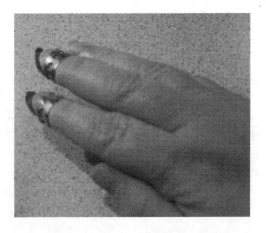

To put on your finger picks, place the fingerprint part of the finger so that it is lying with the dip of the pick, and the point of the pick is at your fingertip.

Most folks want to wear them as if they were fingernails, which seems to make sense—but DON'T! It will rip the strings right off your banjo.

Chords

G

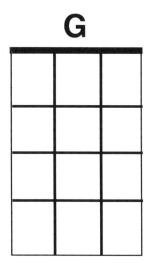

A chord is several notes put together that sound good when played together. Our banjo is tuned to Open G, which means that when we strum across the strings with no fingers on the fretboard, we are automatically playing a G chord. This tends to be the banjo player's favorite chord!

Chord chart is showing only four strings because the fifth string is usually not fretted.

Note: This chord chart is showing no fingers....so this would be a G

Practice with Your G Chord
strum downward with your thumb pick= /

Row Your Boat

G   /   /   /   /   /   /   /

Row row row your boat Gently down the stream

   /   /   /   /   /   /   /   /

Merrily merrily merrily merrily   Life is but a dream

Memorize these chords as you work on them. This will make it easier, as all the songs will usually just have a letter stating the chord you will be using.

D7

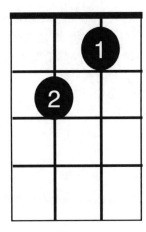

Left-hand fingers:
Thumb: Goes on back of banjo neck
1 = Index finger
2 = Middle finger
3 = Ring finger
4 = Pinky

Our next chord is D7.

When fretting the notes, use only the tips of your fingers, almost to the point that it seems as if the string is going to go under your nail. Yep, that close! You may want to trim your fingernails; they need to be short or the nail will prevent your finger from touching the string, thus making a frustrating "no play" note.

Make sure you place your fingertip right behind the fret. If you place it directly on top of the fret, you will get a buzz.

Let's try our new chord in a song.

Skip to My Lou

G   /   /   /   /   /   /   /
Skip   Skip   Skip to my Lou

D7   /   /   /   /   /   /   /
Skip   Skip   Skip to my Lou

G   /   /   /   /   /   /   /
Skip   Skip   Skip to my Lou

D7   /   /   /   G /   /   /
Skip to my Lou my dar- -ling.

C

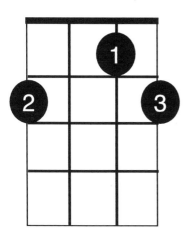

Our last chord is C. Notice the index finger is in the same place as our D7. From there we are going to add fingers on both of the outside strings.

Let's try all of our chords in a song.

Crawdad Song

G / / / / / / / / / / / ////
You get a line and I'll get a po --le hon-ey
 / / / / / / / / D7 / / /////
 You get a line and I'll get a po-le ba   be
 G / / / / / / /
 You get a line and I'll get a pole
 C / / / / / / /
We'll go fishin' in the crawdad hole
 G / / / D7 / / / G / / / / / / /
Honey, oh ba   by...mine

7

Reading Tablature
A Method To Play An Instrument Quickly

It's wonderful to know how to read musical notation—but it can be very time-consuming to learn,
and it comes much easier for younger folks.
Tablature makes it easier and quicker to learn to play music.

Let me show you how tablature works.

Each line represents a string on your banjo.
Note: Remember that your banjo is called a 5-string banjo, with the short string (the one closest to
you) being the fifth string. So count the strings backwards from the fifth string; 5, 4, 3, 2, and 1.

```
String 1  ─────────────────────────────3──────────
String 2  ───────────────────────1────────────────
String 3  ──────────────0──────────────────────────
String 4  ────────2────────────────────────────────
String 5  ───0─────────────────────────────────────
```

Numbers indicate the fret number. The number will be on a specific line
telling you which string to play. The number will tell you which fret to play
on that string.

In the case at the top, the number 2 is located on the 4th string and
indicates the second fret … and so on. Zero (0) means to play the string
"open," or with no fingers.

As we continue, you will notice that some of the songs will be written in
tablature, but will also show rhythm notation of each note.

Practicing Reading Rhythm and Tab

Below is an example of the rhythm we will use in playing the banjo. Not all songs have the same notation, so you'll need to pay close attention to the time signature, which tells you how many beats are in each measure (each individual box).

Quarter notes receive one full beat
Half notes receive two beats
Whole notes receive four beats
Eighth notes are a quarter note cut in half, so they receive one-half beat (each pair receives one beat)

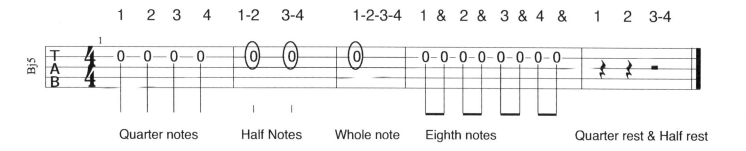

Below is a familiar song written in tab. Take your time as you play. Reminder: the bottom line is your fifth string (short string) which is closest to you. The numbers indicate the frets.

Helpful hint: When playing the banjo, it's best to keep your fingers from getting tangled. Remember this simple pattern:

First/index finger: plays in first fret
Second/middle finger: plays in second fret
Third/ring finger: plays in third fret

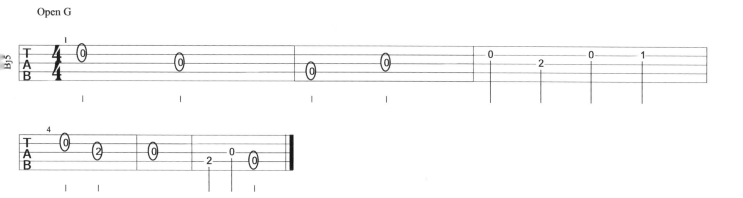

The Basic Up-Picking Pattern

Now it's time to give our playing that "banjoey" sound! Below is the basic up-picking pattern we will be using. Each finger will have only one job, which is one reason this style is so quick and easy to learn. It's also quick and easy to sight-read. First, the notes standing alone are quarter notes, which represent the melody and will be played with the index finger. Second, the notes that are connected are eighth notes and represent the chord/strum, which will be played with your middle finger. Lastly, the single note connected with the chord/strum will be played with your thumb.

As you can see, each finger has its one and only job.

To recap:
Index finger has a finger pick on it, and plays the individual notes or the melody.
Middle finger brushes down on the strings with the back of the fingernail (only brush the strings below the fingernail, no need to move your finger any more than necessary).
Thumb has a thumb pick on it, and plays only the fifth string open. It is always connected with the brush/chord.

Note: in most cases, the melody note will fall right into the chord, which makes playing a piece of cake!

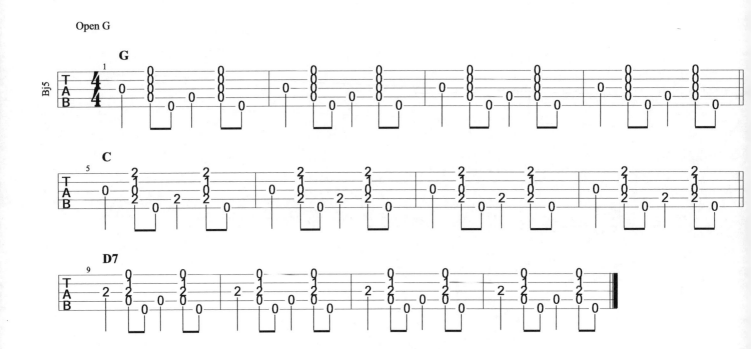

Good Night Ladies

Traditional

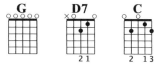

Open G

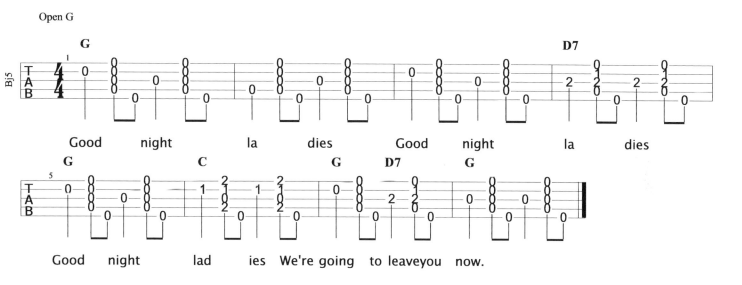

Good   night   la   dies   Good   night   la   dies

Good   night   lad   ies   We're going   to leaveyou   now.

Boil 'Em Cabbage

Traditional

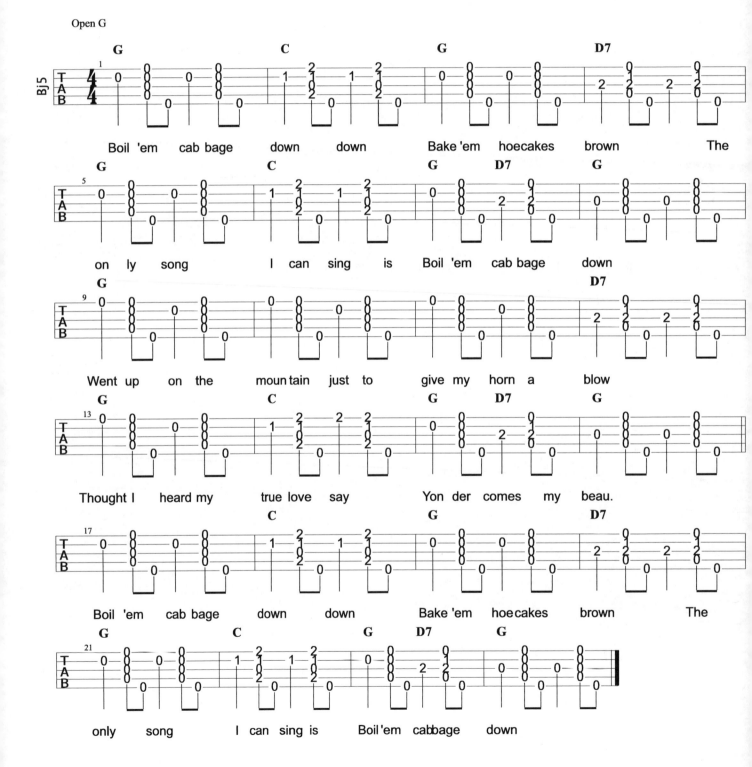

Will the Circle Be Unbroken

Traditional - Level 1

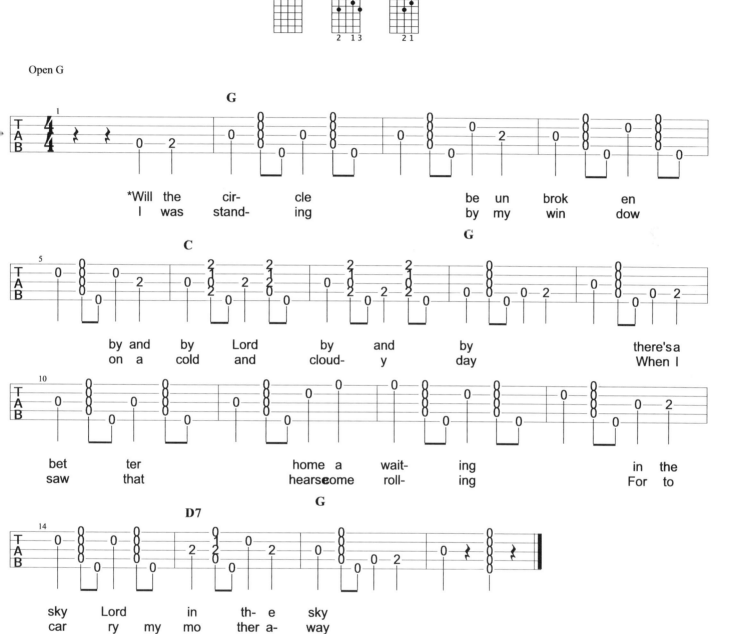

Jesse James

Traditional

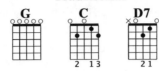

Open G

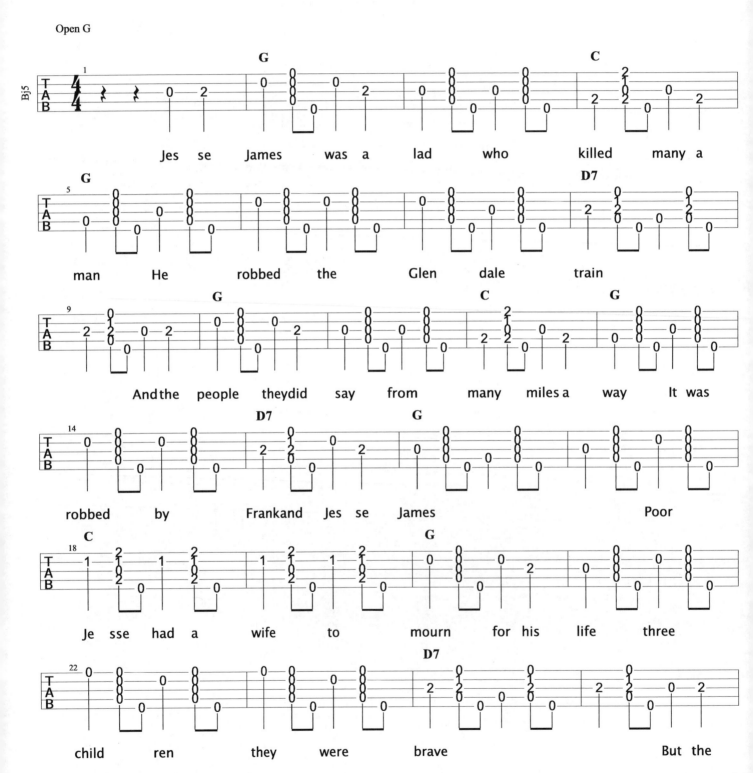

14

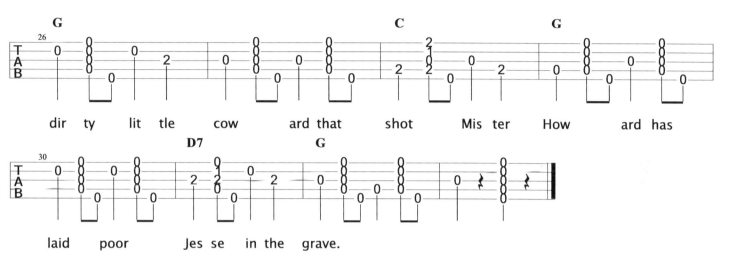

dir ty   lit tle   cow   ard that   shot   Mis ter   How   ard has

laid   poor   Jes se   in the   grave.

I'll Fly Away
Traditional - Level 1

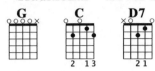

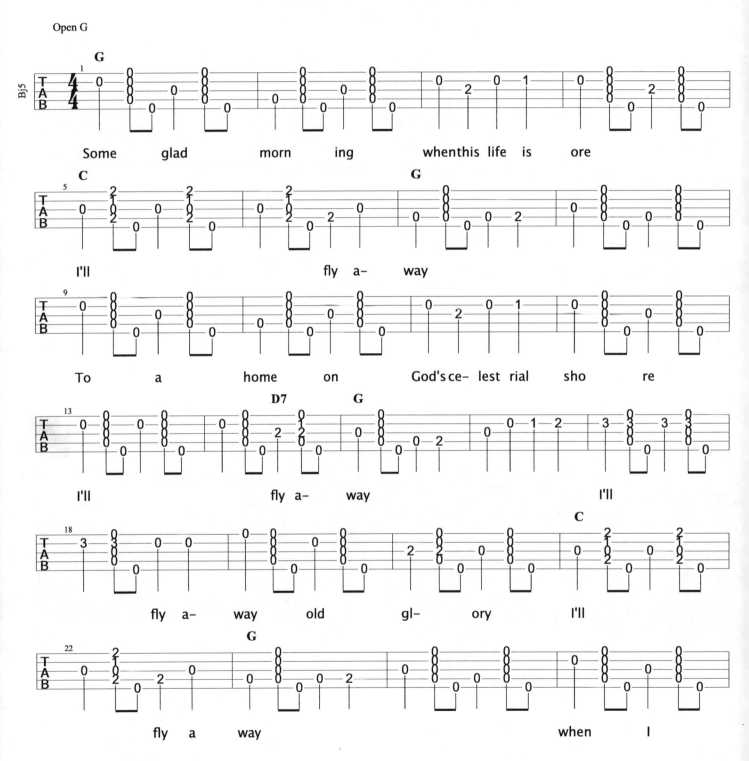

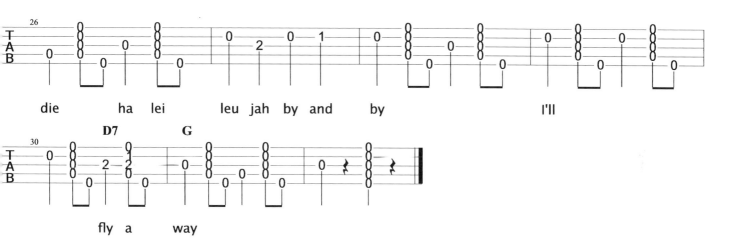

die   ha   lei   leu   jah   by   and   by   I'll

fly   a   way

What a Friend We Have in Jesus

Traditional - Level 1

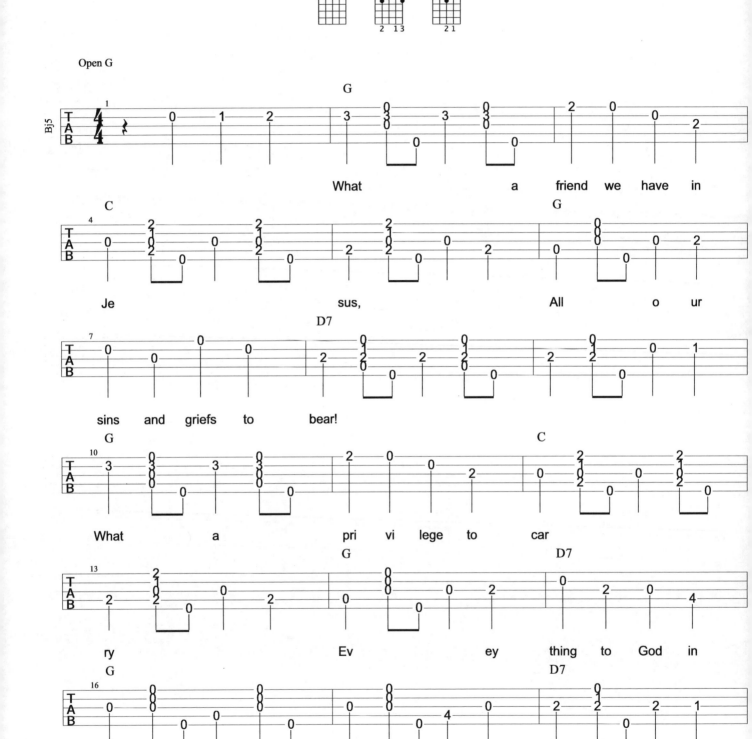

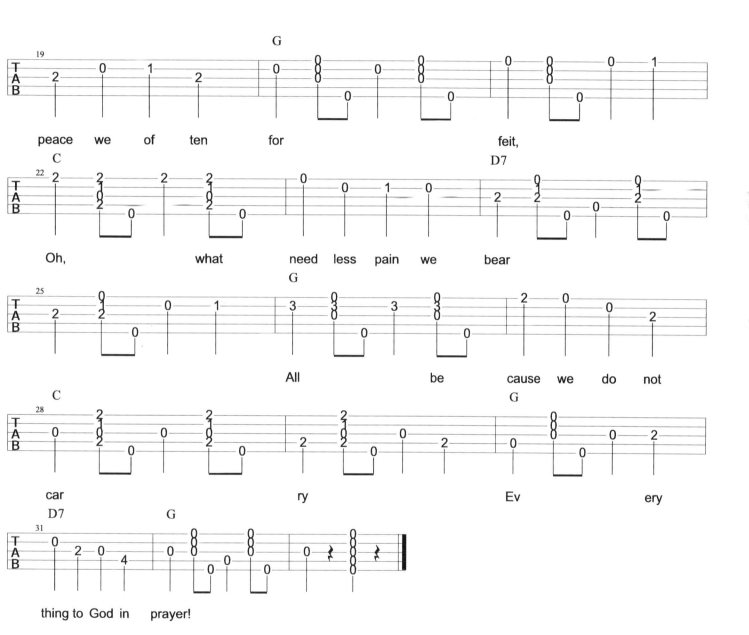

peace   we   of   ten   for   feit,

Oh,   what   need less pain we bear

All   be   cause we do not

car   ry   Ev   ery

thing to God in   prayer!

Banjo Techniques
These give the banjo its distinctive sound

Slide

A slide is a technique that helps make the melody note stand out. It starts on one fret and slides to another fret, but you pluck the string only one time. Don't rush the first note; if you do, it will sound more like "zip." Hold the first note a tad longer; then slide to the next position.

Here are a few common slides.

Common Slides

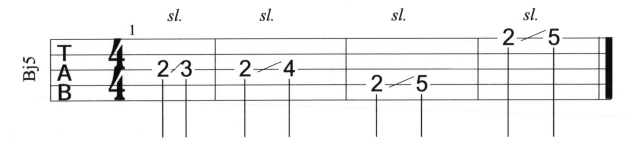

Hammer-On

A hammer-on is similar to a slide, as it also produces two notes with one pluck of the string. With this technique, you will play one note, hold, and then put your finger on the second note which will always be a higher pitch. When you put your finger down to "hammer," you will need to hit it a little harder than normal, much as you may try to run down ants racing across your countertop. If you hit hard enough, the note will be clear and you will hear your finger hitting the fretboard.

Common Hammer-Ons

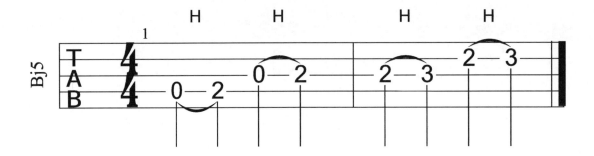

The Pull-Off

The Pull-Off is also similar to the slide and hammer-on, as it too, produces 2 notes from one pluck of the string. A pull off always starts with a higher note, pulling off to a lower note. Again, don't rush the first note or like the others, the notes will just slide into each other, rather than having two distinct notes.

Common Pull-Off's

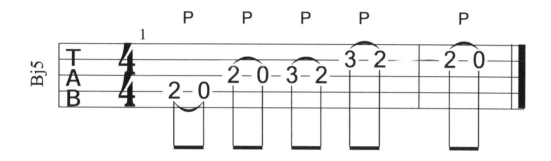

Now that you have an idea of slides, hammer-ons, and pull-offs, let's start using them in some songs!

Let's work thru Cripple Creek!

21

Cripple Creek

Traditional

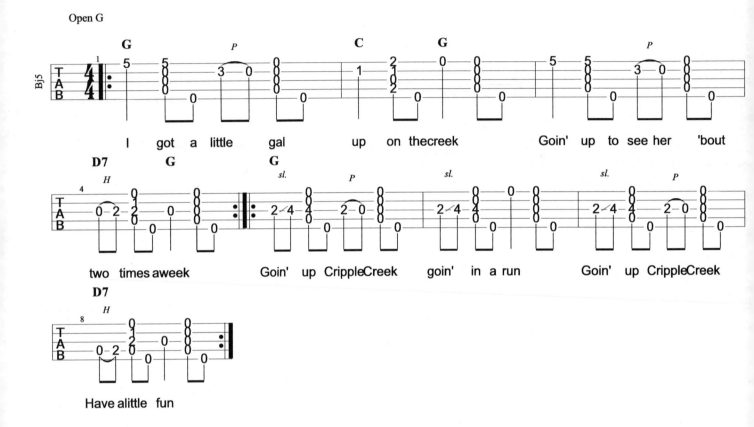

I: and :I are repeat signs

The repeat signs mean you play each verse 2 times

Play the first line thru to the first part of the 2nd line...then go back and play it again. After you play it twice, play the 2nd line thru 2 times.

This is called an AABB song.

Will the Circle Be Unbroken

Traditional - Level 2

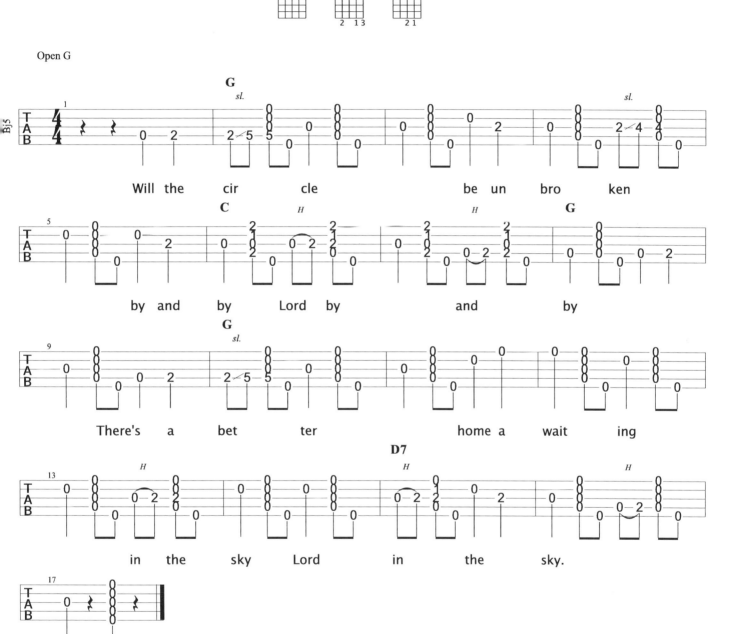

I'll Fly Away

Traditional - Level 2

Open G

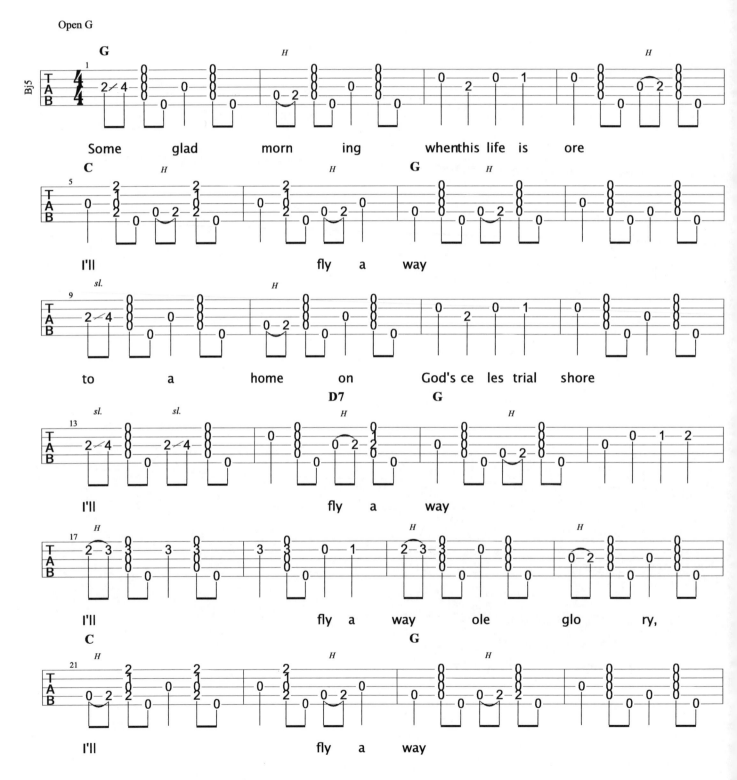

Some glad morn ing when this life is ore

I'll fly a way

to a home on God's ce les trial shore

I'll fly a way

I'll fly a way ole glo ry,

I'll fly a way

24

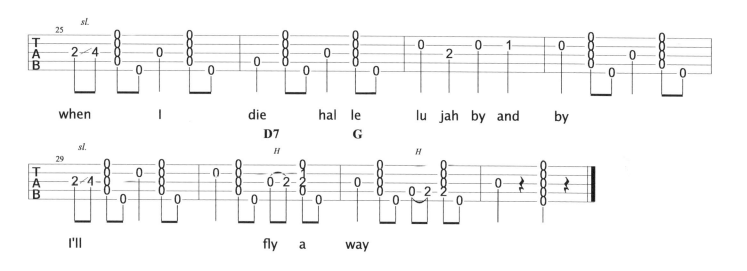

when   I   die   hal le   lu jah by and   by

I'll   fly   a   way

Wildwood Flower

Traditional

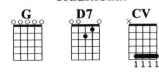

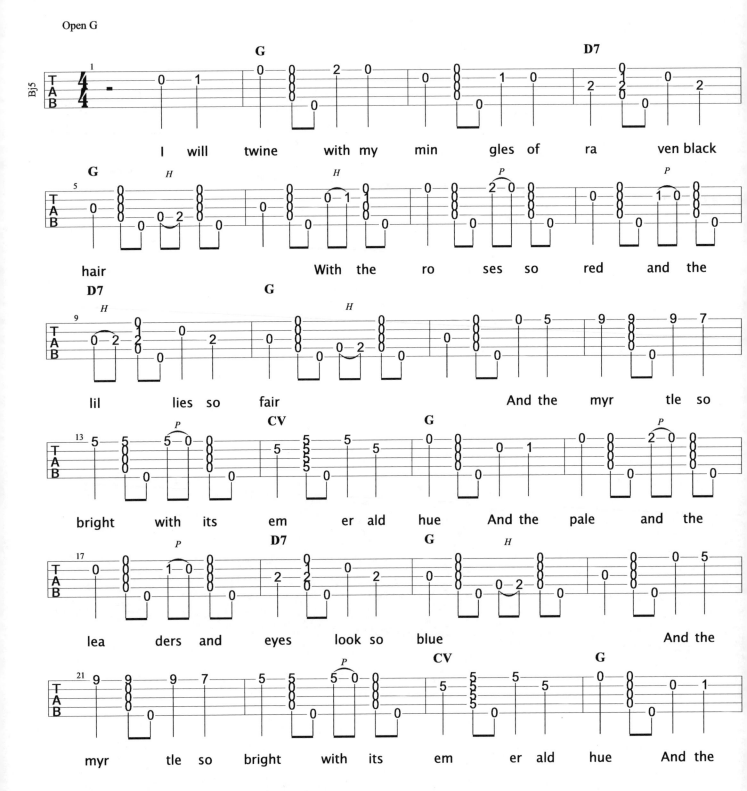

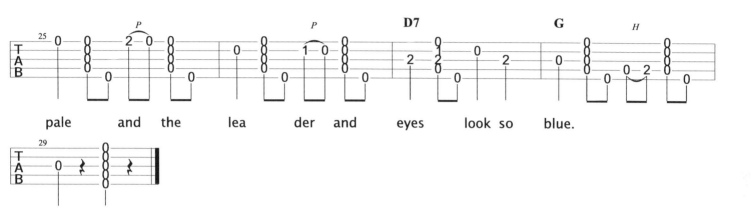

pale   and   the   lea   der and   eyes   look so   blue.

Church in the Wildwood

Traditional

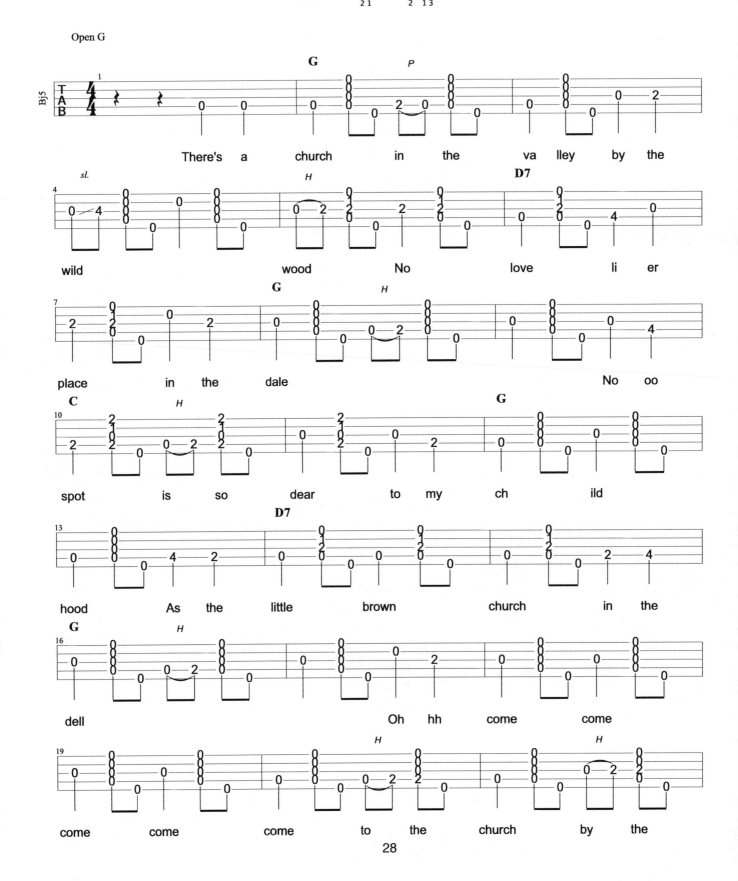

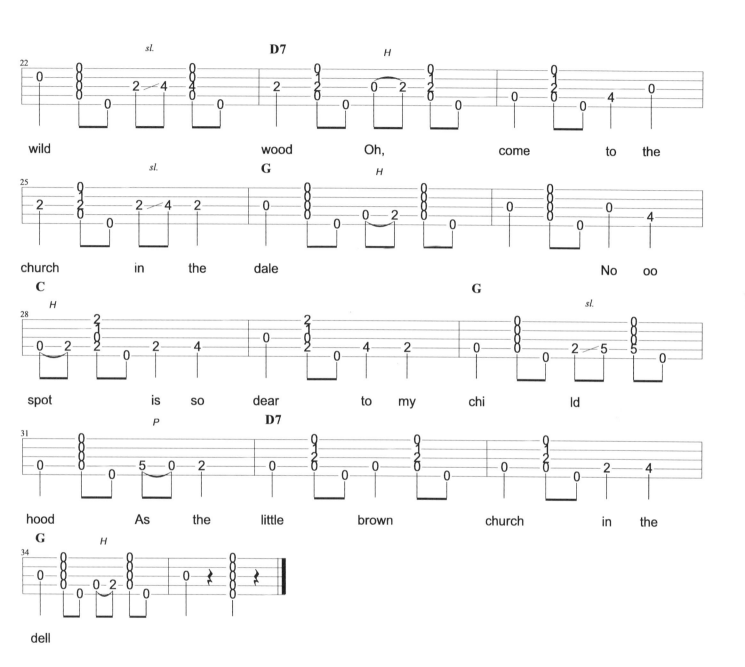

wild   wood   Oh,   come   to   the

church   in   the   dale   No   oo

spot   is   so   dear   to   my   chi   ld

hood   As   the   little   brown   church   in   the

dell

When You and I were Young, Maggie

Traditional

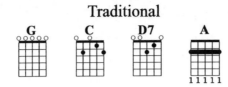

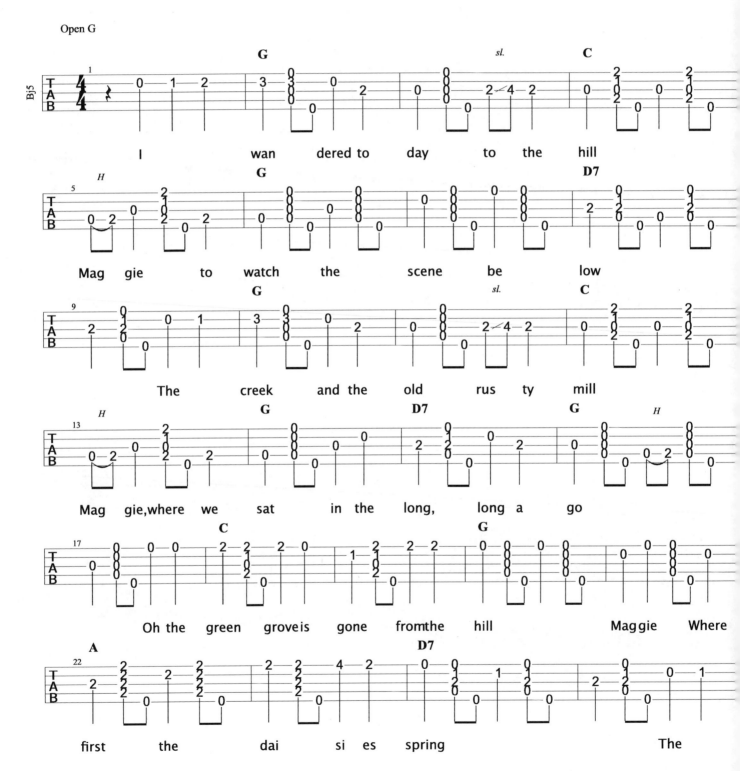

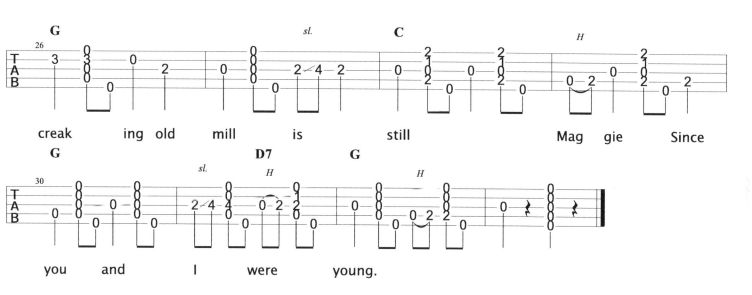

creak   ing old mill   is   still   Mag gie   Since

you   and   I   were   young.

Old Joe Clark

Traditional

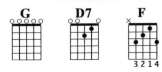

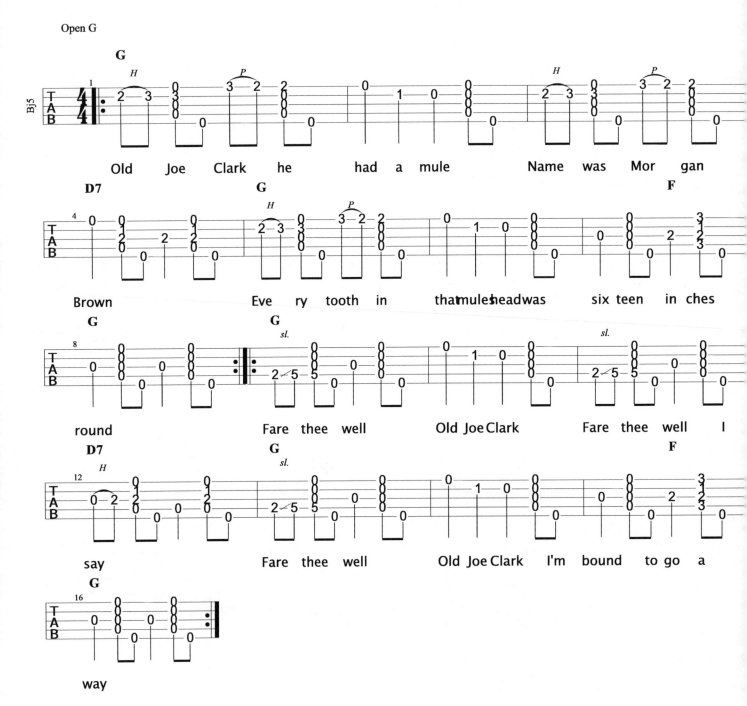

Old   Joe   Clark   he   had   a   mule   Name   was   Mor   gan

Brown   Eve   ry   tooth   in   that mule head was   six teen   in ches

round   Fare   thee   well   Old Joe Clark   Fare   thee   well   I

say   Fare   thee   well   Old Joe Clark   I'm   bound   to   go   a

way

Accompanying Yourself on the Banjo

So now you know how to play the song; but what if the song has words, and you want to sing as well as play it? It's easy! Instead of playing the melody, you can play one of these patterns to accompany yourself as you sing!

Let's say one of your favorite songs is Wildwood Flower, but you would really like to sing the lyrics. Instead of playing the complete melody on the banjo, which would be too "busy" as you are singing the words, you can play a particular and familiar pattern. For example, the pattern below would work great when you are singing the words to Wildwood Flower!

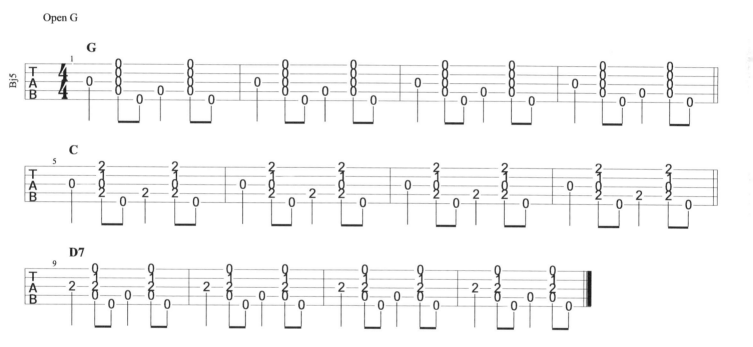

This is called an alternating bass pattern. Notice that the strings that are plucked are always the third and fourth strings. It is called the alternating bass pattern because these are the two lowest notes on the banjo. It alternates between two notes, with the second note always the lowest note.

Just remember, the two strings that are plucked always remain the same. The only thing that changes is your chord! Easy enough!

Wildwood Flower Singing Accompaniment

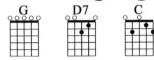

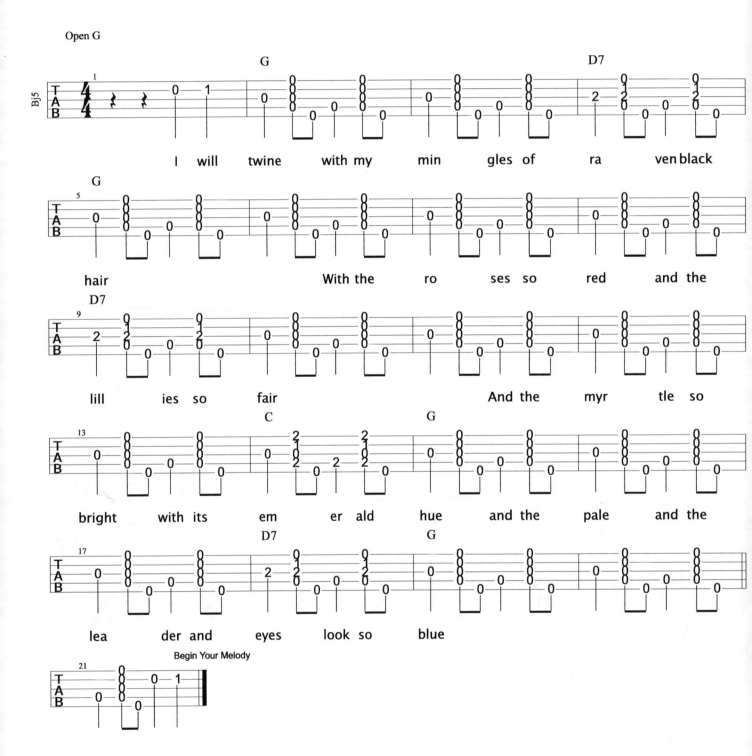

Accompaniment Patterns in 4/4 Time

Open G

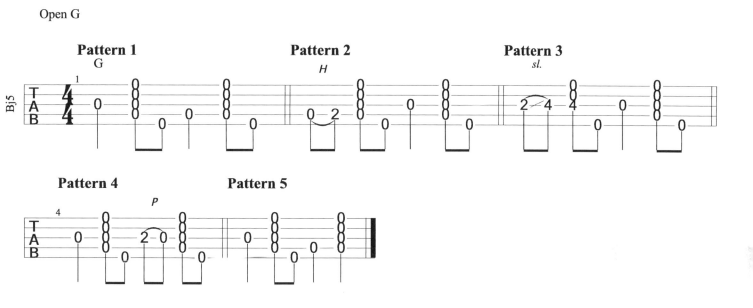

Accompaniment Patterns in 3/4 Time

Open G

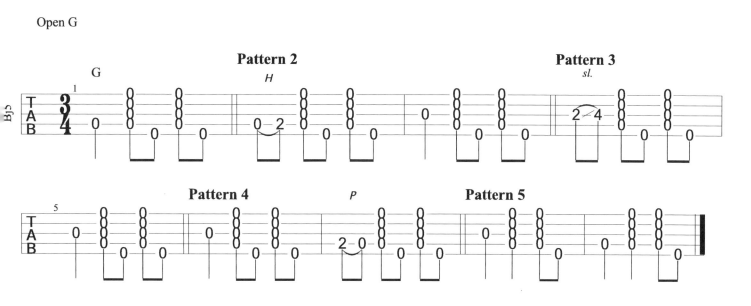

Photo by: Jade Reese Photography

Anna E. Uptain specializes in Group Lessons for Adult Beginners in guitar, banjo, mandolin and ukulele and has taught thru The University of Tennessee, Pellissippi State Technical College, Calhoun State Community College, ORICL - Oak Ridge Institute for Continued Learning, The Knoxville Center for Crafts and Fine Arts, The Museum of Appalachia as well as having classes at her own studio. You can also find Anna teaching school groups about Appalachian music and history, as well as being a touring performer, singer and musician!

She picked up the guitar at age 12 and soon moved to the banjo at 15 and began playing in local gospel groups in her hometown of Columbia, Tennessee. Mandolin also came into the picture, but really "didn't take" until her adult years.

Anna earned her Bachelor's of Music Degree in Music Education and Church Music from Lambuth University. After several years of "trying to find her musical niche", she began teaching full time lessons in 2000.

You can find classes with Anna online at: www.fretsalive.com.

Copyright © 2010
Anna E. Uptain
Knoxville, TN 37921
www.fretsalive.com
Email: fretsalive@me.com
All rights reserved. No reproduction without permission.

66099769R00022

Made in the USA
San Bernardino, CA
08 January 2018